YOU'RE A REAL WINE LOVER WHEN...

Bert Witte

The Wine Appreciation Guild
San Francisco

The Wine Appreciation Guild Ltd.
360 Swift Ave.
South San Francisco, CA 94080
1 800 231-9463
www.wineappreciation.com

ISBN 1-891267-25-6

Translation: Marian Nuis, English Caption Editorial Team: John Cesano, Chad Elder,
Bryan Imelli, Elliott Mackey, Jim Mackey, Alex Shaw, Steve Watkins.

English Typesetting: Diane Spencer Hume

Printed in the United States of America

CONTENTS

You're a real wine-lover when...

...you're not afraid to drink and dress.

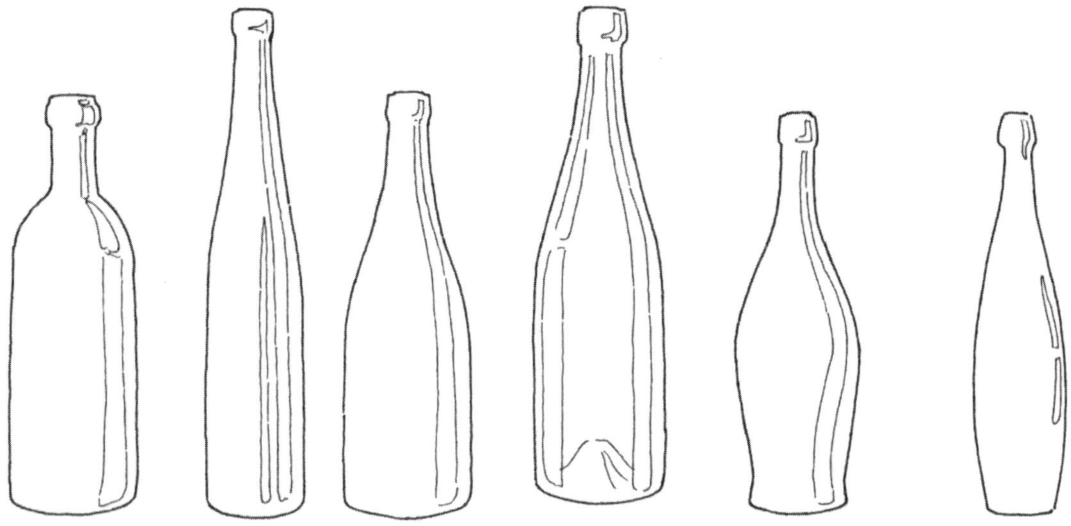

A B C D E F

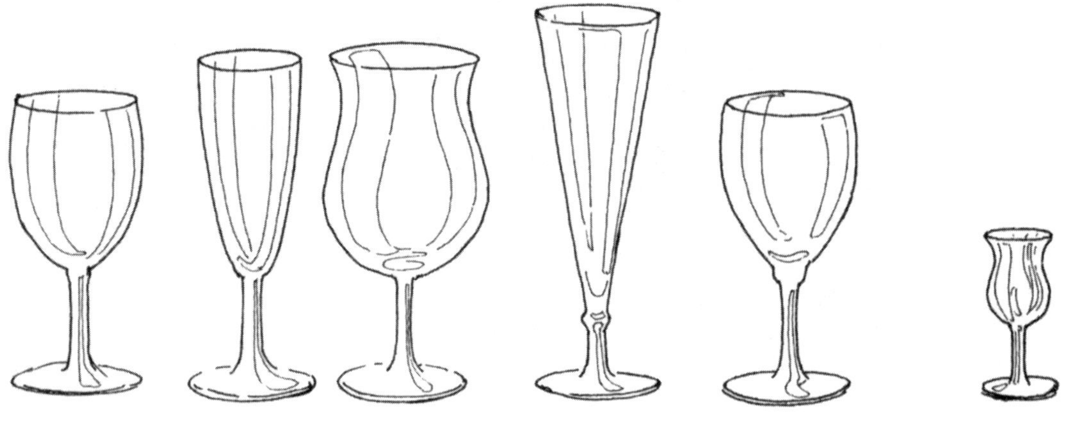

Aa Bb Cc Dd Ee Ff

You're a real wine-lover when…

In order to help the coming wine lover, wine buyer, wine sampler and wine drinker, on the afore page the various bottles for the particular wines are shown, together with the types of glasses to be used for drinking them.

    A.   Bordeaux
    B.   Alsace
    C.   Bourgogne
    D.   Champagne
    E.   Rosé Jura/Provence
    F.   Bowling pin

After emptying the glass (Ff) shown beneath, you will see the bowling pin (F) automatically.

…you can determine from the bottle and the glass which way the 'wine' blows…

You're a real wine-lover when...

...you use wine in your personal hygiene.

You're a real wine-lover when...

...you have great wine war-stories.

You're a real wine-lover when...

...you drink only wines of high ranking labels.

You're a real wine-lover when...

...you get bored with wine tasting and engage in other contests of skill.

You're a real wine-lover when...

...you will even volunteer to judge bad wines.

You're a real wine-lover when...

...you quickly react to the taste of T.C.A*

(*If you are a real wine lover you know what T.C.A. is)

A NEAT AND COLORFUL WINE, SOMEWHAT MODEST IN CHARACTER, BUT NEVERTHE-
LESS OF A ROBUST ORIGIN, WITH A LIGHT, SPRING-LIKE, FRESH-FRUITY TOUCH
WITH SOME CHERRY, NO, RATHER APRICOT, ALMOST CHERRY, WHAT AM I BAB-
BLING, I SHOULD SAY NECTARINE WITH A SUBTLE LIGHT SMELL OF CANDIES
AS WELL AS A NUTTY FLAVOR UNDER ONE'S TONGUE, A LIGHT TOUCH OF OAK,
NATURALLY, HALF A YEAR ON BARREL DOESN'T PASS UNNOTICED, BUT THEN SU-
PERBLY OVAL ON THE TASTE BUDS, AND...O, O, O, SUCH A MIGHTY OVERPOWER-
ING PERFUME, TERRIFIC THE WAY IT ROARS THROUGH YOUR NOSE, ALTHOUGH...A
TRIFLE TOO PENETRATING, PITY, PITY, ALTHOUGH... DO I TASTE A MOUTHFUL
OF RICH CALCAREOUS SOIL, A SOUTH-BY-SOUTHEASTERLY MOUNTAIN SLOPE, YES,
WELL NO, YES, YES, NO...AHHH...NO DON'T SAY ANYTHING YET, YEA...HMMM...NO,
NOT SO, OR YET SO, DEUCED, OF COURSE, I SHOULD HAVE THOUGHT OF IT
BEFORE, LOOK AT THE COLOR: WARMLY SPARKLING AND SHINING IT HANGS TO
THE GLASS, INTENSELY RED, SCARLET I WOULD SAY, OR RATHER RUBY, THAT'S
IT ALTHOUGH, PURPLE-RUBY MORE CLOSELY, LET'S SAY SCARLETPURPLERUBY, MY
MY, SUCH CLASS, SUCH REGAL SIMPLICITY, MAJESTICALLY, ...AHH GENIALLY,
RIGHT, PRECISELY, EXACTLY, THAT'S IT: A REGAL, MAGISTRAL, GENIAL WINE,
UNBELIEVABLE.

You're a real wine-lover when...

...you actually believe that women are interested in what you have to say about wine.

You're a real wine-lover when...

...your friends call you "Mr. Corkscrew."

You're a real wine-lover when...

...you know the secret language of wine tasting.

You're a real wine-lover when…

…you require a full glass before rejecting a 1945 Lafite.

You're a real wine-lover when…

…you really get into your wine…

You're a real wine-lover when…

…your final request is a blind tasting.

You're a real wine-lover when…

…you're modest in showing your wine knowledge.

You're a real wine-lover when...

...you specialize in blind tastings.

You're a real wine-lover when...

...you enjoy all the glamour of your own vineyard.

You're a real wine-lover when…

…you even give your body to the crush.

You're a real wine-lover when...

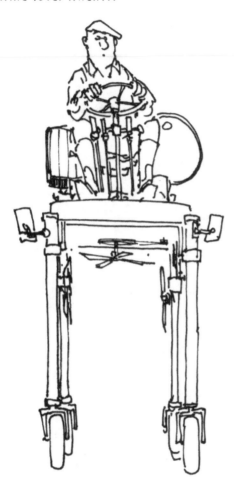

…you make personal use of the vineyard equipment.

You're a real wine-lover when...

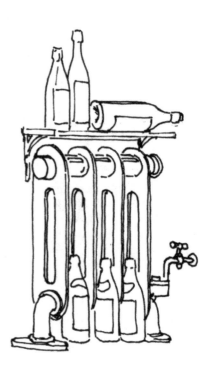

...you know how to turn good wine into vinegar.

You're a real wine-lover when…

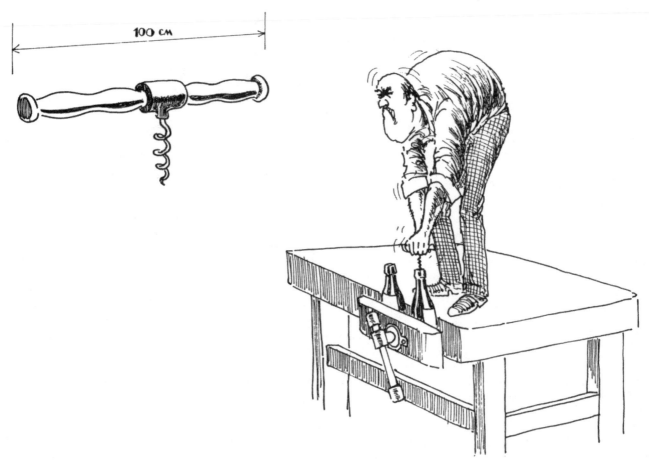

100 CM

…you have the right tool for every bottle.

You're a real wine-lover when...

...you know how to bring red wine to room temperature.

You're a real wine-lover when...

...you know how to make your own ice wine.

You're a real wine-lover when...

...you are familiar with the micro-climates of your apartment.

You're a real wine-lover when...

...you know how to marinate your game the "French Way"

You're a real wine-lover when…

…you tolerate cooking with wine in your home.

You're a real wine-lover when...

... you're suspicious of Riesling made in Algeria.

You're a real wine-lover when...

...you can point out to the Sommelier his small selection of wines.

You're a real wine-lover when...

...you can argue about oak content with the best of experts

You're a real wine-lover when...

…you know how to handle the Sommelier in the best of places.

You're a real wine-lover when...

...you know where to get complete wine service.

You're a real wine-lover when…

…you know how to be a good guest after a few glasses of wine.

You're a real wine-lover when…

…you are willing to share your best wines with your mother-in-law.

You're a real wine-lover when…

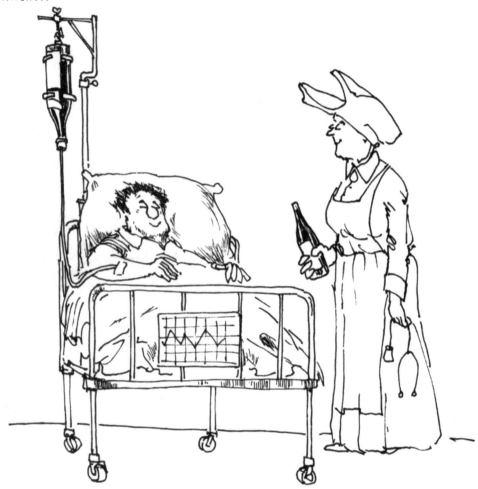

…you get the best of medicines in the hospital.

You're a real wine-lover when...

...even after a few glasses of wine, your date still looks beautiful.

You're a real wine-lover when...

...you are recognized in your neighborhood as an avid recycler.

You're a real wine-lover when…

…your neighbor beats you to the last bottle of your "secret wine discovery."

You're a real wine-lover when...

...you select the church where the sacramental wine is a vintage first growth and the prayer ends with Cheers.

You're a real wine-lover when...

...you even store your car in French Oak!

You're a real wine-lover when...

...you're a music lover too, particularly of Johann Sebastian Bacchus.

You're a real wine-lover when...

...you have too little blood in your alcohol.

You're a real wine-lover when…

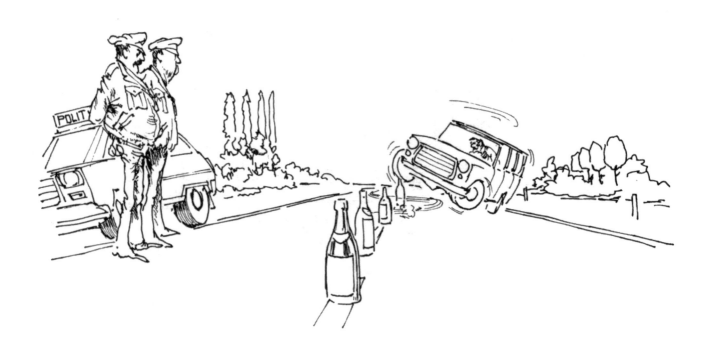

…you convince the police that you're practicing for the new Olympic bottle slalom.

You're a real wine-lover when...

...you insist on making your own wine out of anything at any cost.

You're a real wine-lover when...

...when your cork floor cost more than the house.

You're a real wine-lover when...

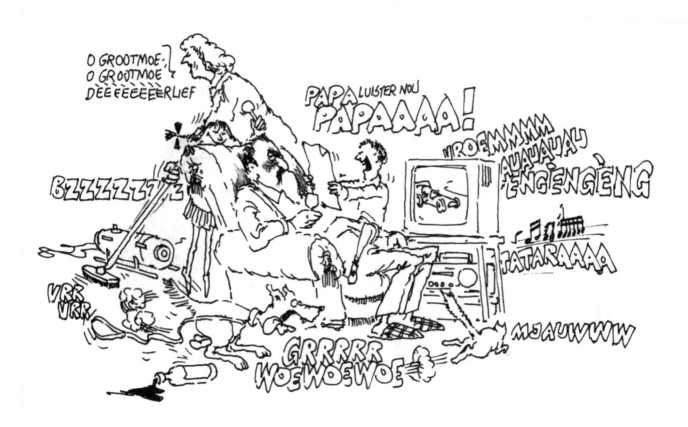

...you can enjoy your wine in the comfort of your own home.

You're a real wine-lover when…

…in times of distress, you know what is most important.

You're a real wine-lover when…

…you enjoy a little "Wine, Women and Song."

You're a real wine-lover when…

…you long for the days before the 100 point scoring systems.

You're a real wine-lover when...

...you have come a long way in the enjoyment of your privacy.

You're a real wine-lover when…

…you collect increasingly larger "bottles."

You're a real wine-lover when...

...as a wine-loving doctor, you know how to "help" your patients.

You're a real wine-lover when...

...you can hear the "sound of wine" under the most difficult conditions.

You're a real wine-lover when...

...you don't let your wife's white carpet in your living room deter you.

Look for These Other WINE APPRECIATION GUILD Titles

The best books for the wine novice...

RED & WHITE, Wine Made Simple by Max Allen. ISBN 1-891267-37-X, $24.95

COMMONSENSE BOOK OF WINE. "The Only Book that Demystifies Wine Without Destroying the Magic." ISBN 0-932664-76-8, $8.95

The best books for wine professionals...

THE UNIVERSITY WINE COURSE, A Wine Appreciation Text and Self Tutorial by Marian Baldy, Ph.D. ISBN 0-932664-69-5, $35.00

THE TASTE OF WINE, The Art and Science of Wine Appreciation by Emile Peynaud. ISBN 0-932664-64-4, $39.95

The best for wine history...

A CENTURY OF WINE, "The Story of a Wine Revolution" by Stephen Brook. ISBN 1-891267-33-7, $50.00

WINE HERITAGE, "The Story of Italian-American Vintners" by Dick Rosano. ISBN 1-891267-13-2, $29.95

The one best wine book ever!

THE GLOBAL ENCYCLOPEDIA OF WINE, "The monumental wine book of the decade", by Rebecca Chapa, Catherine Fallis MS, Patrick Farrell, MW and 33 additional wine authorities. ISBN 1-891267-38-8, $75.00